VOICES IN THE VOID

SNEHA RANA

Made with ♥ on the Notion Press Platform
www.notionpress.com

To everyone who's trying...

Contents

Contents

Contents

Preface

Like every teenager, I too have my share of days when I want to burn down the paperhouse around me and when I struggle to express what I feel and when there's no reason I see and all I want is to be free.

Poetry, for me, has been a tool of momentary escapsim. Something that helps me to understand, to let go, to make sense of what's going on, to comprehend my thoughts and my actions.

To write, is to bleed and so it goes... "If you never bleed you're never gonna grow."

~Taylor Swift

Acknowledgements

I would like to appreciate maa and papa for providing me with the oppurtunity to do this. I also gratefully acknowledge the support of my friends without which I dont know what would be of me. Thank You.

1. Day 1

I am the dust
under your feet
With freedom to go
but your imprints on me
Carve out your name
etched in pure gold
Slipping down your hands
hold on to let go

2. Day 2

Bring myself down,
Scale your heights,
Tell me what must I do
to keep you looking at me
Turning all the tables,
Burning the blue sky,
I'll be on my knees
over ruins of me

3. Day 3

I'm as good as gone
that's what it is
to be in my shoes.
Hiding away
avoiding plain sight
and just like a ghost
I live in moonlight.
I'm told,
I'm not spoken to
I'm related
to people I don't relate to.
The only voices I hear
are shrill banshees
echoing from the walls
and I give in

4. Day 4

Everything within me
collapses to ruins
With every scream
I'm nowhere to be seen
The muffled cries
of my deconstructed soul
Grasps the conscience
and doesn't let go

5. Day 5

Breaking my bones
to build your pedestal
Look down at me,
see right through
Think about how spiteful
my mannerism is
Turn a blind eye
to what you do
Haze on my heart
not a word spoken
Taking what I'm given
in hopes of changing what's true

6. Day 6

I am not whole anymore
like I once was
Reminiscing the misses pieces
of innocence that are lost
Parts of me were killed
in the house I grew up in,
by the people I grew up around,
with time that passed

7. Day 7

Do you hear my screams
tearing through your soul
Do you see what's behind
the tactics that seem old
Do you feel my breath
on the nape of your neck
Do you sense me staring
when the dawn cracks

I'm there
Captivated, yet so free
Everywhere you go
you'll find me

8. Day 8

Can someone
show me the right way
I try to
create my own
But I'm told to
walk on the one once made

9. Day 9

Let me cry
don't ask why
Don't tell me to speak
Look in my eyes
Isn't it clear?
Don't you see?
I'm tired
and for the last time
I gather
whatever remains
and scream
I don't have it in me
To go on …

10. Day 10

How do I forgive
Myself?
for every version I could've been
for every tear I could've prevented
for every night I could've slept tight
How do I forgive
Myself?
for every cloud of self doubt
for every lost opportunity
for every insecurity
How do I forgive
Myself?
for the grief that still haunts
for the guilt that still flaunts
for the dark in my day
that'll probably never go away

11. Day 11

You don't know
how bad it hurts,
To put your best foot forward
and get slam dunked.
To do all you could and yet
end up with posters
of what you didn't do right
and why you're never gonna be enough.
All the places you lack
are painted neon
for everyone to see, mock and leave
you hanging low and grasping
every breath you can
before the skies open up
and the clouds bestow you
with whatever sympathy they have
for your little brittle heart

12. Day 12

Yes, there were fragments
that got lost on the way
Yes, there were versions
Which I can't yet say
Yes there were complications
and mistakes were made

Don't see the parts, that were swept
but see how much of me is left

13. Day 13

I wake up
sweaty and panting
the demons in my nightmares
with their bewitching glares
are coming to me
from deep within
a place long lost
and almost forgotten about

14. Day 14

Dreams of living
Splashing spectrum on my grave
Let me cry
It's what the hole in me craves
Been long enough with the pretence
I still hold on to the illusion of my existence
Death will numb the pain
I must succumb
To the injuries that
Cannot be seen
But are visible only
To the eyes of the willing

15. Day 15

I plead.
You let it pass away,
look at me
and rip the bandages off
Right when I try
to hide in the crowd
I'm dragged on the stage
to face the guilt
that comes with being me

16. Day 16

Tell me,
what does a perishing pigeon symbolize?
With its half open eyes,
blood curdling cries
that no one can hear
It takes it breath by breath
the beginning of the end
Its panting heavily,
there's nothing I can do
It looks my way, I look away
I can't sit here doing nothing
Oh but I have to
It feels wrong
to look in its eyes
and wish with tears
that it dies

We've all been there
half dead or half alive,
Does it matter?

17. Day 17

Dancing around
all of my what if's
Back and forth
making the lines blurry
Insanity, to me comes easil
Don't need to pretend
that I am seen

Can broken dandelions
really carry the weight of hopes?

18. Day 18

But how can anyone trust
in a world
Where no one is
who they say they are
Where no one shows
their true intentions
Where no one strives
for peace and kind
Where no thrives
without derision and lies
Where no one likes
the truth spoken aloud
Where the heart is
merely a dark cloud

19. Day 19

Looking in the mirror
my mind wanders
I'm an island
So abundant
With the aspect of beauty
Fulfilling the needs of vary passerby's
No one stops to discover
what's hidden from plain sight
Secrets within withering
the soul that holds my being
Crumbling existence
in the middle of the nowhere sea

20. Day 20

If people were rain

I'd be a downpour

Soaking to the bones

leaving no traces in the aftermath

The deeper you look

my melancholy you observe

Pouring out parts of me

to spite smiles on surrounding faces

21. Day 21

Whispers
In the dark
"You won't last.
Soon
You'll see
You'll be in the past"
"Hypocrite"
It screams
With posters on the walls
I pace back and forth
But no one picks up my calls

22. Day 22

My breath gets caught
In my throat
Standing on shaky ground
I can expect nothing more
Just when I think I'm over it
It comes back and leaves me sore
All my fears come from me
And what remains will be passed on
I can feel myself falling
Lost in my own thoughts
I'm drowning in the high tides
Sat like a stone and I cried
Oh no..
Oh no..
It's happening all over again

23. Day 23

I'd like to walk around in my mind
to see where I come from
to know why am I left here
staring at the January stars
tangled in the blues
choking on crimson flowers

24. Day 24

Now that you're gone
I'll light up candles of your name
Write letters with my blood
And cry on your grave
Are falling stars so beautiful
because they're broken?

25. Day 25

Shut the door
Turn the shower on
Look at me
Standing on the other side
3 seconds pass
Now I'm on the floor
Wet clothes
No light in my eyes

26. Day 26

Like the phases of the moon
I ask myself
Which part of him will I meet today?
Will he make me smile?
Like good old times
Will I shut my eyes and sleep?
Seeing a stranger cross his lines

27. Day 27

Faced my blues,
looked you in the eye
Days and days
of drowning in my tears
Will it be enough?
if my sun never shines too brightly
Will it be okay?
if I can only promise you thunder
Will it be fine?
if someday my battleships died at war
Will it be okay?
if my rain soaks you to the core
I don't belong, but oh, I'm reduced
to bringing ridicule at the table

28. Day 28

Push me away
you're doing a great job
I try to fill the void
you show me why I should not
I feel paralyzed
every time you look at me
With those gray eyes.
I don't know how to fix us
I don't know if I should
Maybe it'll be better
if I stayed out of your woods
I spend my nights trying to undo
the wear and tear your words do
My treacherous heart breaks
and I cry myself to sleep
Time and time again...

29. Day 29

You call out my bluff,
paint my lies neon
The smile of satisfaction,
burns down my paper house
I step aside,
wiping my eyes
My heart up in flames
dying a million little times

30. Day 30

I was never scared
Of the monsters under my bed
Cause there were none
They're all in my head.
The voices never stop
I can't tell what's true;
Bleeding me dry
Till I don't recognize
The faintly familiar silhouette,
The half alive lie

31. Day 31

Bolted the doors of my heart
Locked him out forever
The paralyzing moment he looked at me
With unrecognition in his eyes
As if our paths never crossed
As if my life was a lie
The breaking of an illusion
Broke more than just my heart

32. Day 32

Like the secrets of the sea
I search for answers
In her eyes
Will I see the fearless maiden?
Bestowed with unknown resilience
Or will I catch a glimpse
Of someone
Who made excuses for the worst?

33. Day 33

On a night with thousand eyes
underneath the streetlights
dancing with the moonlight
I scream
I exist! I exist! I exist!

34. Day 34

And when the clock strikes five
Everything goes cold inside
I'm here
On a February night
Once again
Wondering if I'll make it in time

35. Day 35

Look at you little one
being comforted just by the thoughts
Of apologies that are never gonna come
by just a ghost of warmth
that lifts the weight off your chest
by just a glint on starlight
that shoes what you're worth
by the tears running down your neck
that promise you'll never bleed again
by wanting to be cradled
by the same hands that tore you apart
by aching to go back
to the ones who once felt like home

36. Day 36

There's a ghost in my house
Her screams
echo although the night
Her touch lingers
for just a little too long
and I find her
wailing
down on her knees
aching
I hold her hand
And walk towards the light

37. Day 37

Search in the lifeless days
Look for me over the moon
Maybe in the ashen nights
Maybe in the afternoons
Check under the rainbows
Peek in the rain soaked clouds
I say I wanna disappear
But all I wanna be is found

38. Day 38

I look for a way
To make your ways hurt less
You fill my heart
With the same old dread
But I'm not afraid now
One day I'll be gone
And never look back

39. Day 39

And when you smile
Tell everyone you're fine
Bite your lips
To avoid crying
Take a deep breath
and count to five
The familiar ache
settles in your chest
Yet you go on
Trying your best

40. Day 40

I still struggle to breathe
Your face clear in the crowd
My wretched heart is wrung
My screams make no sound
I hope we'd never met
You're a shape shifter
And here I'm left
In a fool's paradise
With skeletons in my closet

41. Day 41

Sometimes

When we're laughing

I hold on to the glimpses

Of what we could be

What we can have

But just like that

It vanishes in thin air

And I'm left

A bit more emptier than last time

42. Day 42

Looking at her
my heart screams
"Give me a reason!"
Our makeshift relationship
Keeps me from living
Teach me your ways
To be oblivious
Don't you set fire to my forest
I'll be in the ashes
To gather what's left of me

43. Day 43

It still lingers
The breathlessness
The echoes
The madness
I think someone died here
It still lingers
The cries
The pretending
The grief
I think someone died here

I haven't met all of me
And yet I shred whatever remains

44. Day 44

I remember being nine
Waking up in the middle of the night
Realizing for the first time
That you won't be her forever
Do you recall? I climbed
Up your bed and hugged you tight
You woke up and I cried
So hard my chest hurt
Did you see? All night
The little girl help on tight
Not wanting to let go, in hindsight
Now we're down to ashes

45. Day 45

And after smiling all day
And being with the people I love
I creep into my bed
Stare at the stars
And drown in my tears

46. Day 46

Its 2:24, past midnight
With tired red eyes
I realize
That everything I've got
Is someday gonna be gone
I wish I'd never grown up
I wish there still were bright colors to see
Life was pretty
when I believed in everything
And everyone believed in me

47. Day 47

Screaming
for whatever its worth
Let me go!
Let me come home!
Don't take me away from myself
And hold me captive
Throwing my heart like a plaything
Why don't you see
The rivers you make me bleed
The ache in my being
While you look right through me

48. Day 48

If only
blue could be happiness
The butterflies on my bruised heart
Could rest in peace
And maybe then
I would be the happiest I've ever been

www.ingramcontent.com/pod-product-compliance
Lightning Source LLC
Chambersburg PA
CBHW031807150726
47989CB00006B/2922